DISCOVER Minerals

by Patricia Brinkman

Table of Contents

Introduction 2
Chapter 1 What Are Minerals? 4
Chapter 2 What Are Minerals Like? 8
Chapter 3 Where Do People Find Minerals? ... 14
Conclusion 18
Concept Map 20
Glossary 22
Index 24

Introduction

People know about **minerals**. People know minerals are everywhere.

Words to Know

crystals

gems

metals

minerals

rocks

solids

See the Glossary on page 22.

Chapter 1

What Are Minerals?

Minerals are old.

▲ This mineral is old.

Minerals are **solids**.

▲ This mineral is solid.

Minerals are in **rocks**.

▲ This mineral is in a rock.

Minerals are not alive.

▲ This mineral is not alive.

Chapter 1

Minerals are in the ground.

▲ Minerals are in the ground.

Minerals are in caves.

Did You Know?
Minerals are natural. Things nature makes are natural. Things people make are not natural.

▲ Minerals are in this cave.

What Are Minerals?

Some minerals are **metals**.

▲ This mineral is a metal.

Some minerals are **gems**.

▲ This mineral is a gem.

Chapter 2

What Are Minerals Like?

Some minerals make marks.

▲ This mineral makes marks.

All minerals break.

▲ This mineral broke.

▲ This mineral broke.

Chapter 2

Some minerals are hard.

▲ This mineral is hard.

Some minerals are soft.

Did You Know?
People put minerals in order. Soft minerals are first. Hard minerals are last.

▲ This mineral is soft.

What Are Minerals Like?

Some minerals are shiny.

▲ This mineral is shiny.

Some minerals are dull.

▲ This mineral is dull.

Chapter 2

Some minerals are colorful.

▲ This mineral is green.

What Are Minerals Like?

Some minerals are **crystals**.

▲ This mineral is crystals.

Chapter 3

Where Do People Find Minerals?

People find minerals in food.

Did You Know?
Cereal has minerals. People add minerals to cereal. People add iron to cereal.

▲ Some minerals are in food.

People find minerals in the sea.

▲ **Some minerals are in the sea.**

Chapter 3

People find minerals in the ground.

▲ Some minerals are in the ground.

Where Do People Find Minerals?

People find minerals in mines.

▲ Some minerals are in mines.

Conclusion

People know many things about minerals. People know what minerals are. People know where to find minerals.

19

Concept Map

Minerals

What Are Minerals?

- old
- solids
- in rocks
- not alive
- in the ground
- in caves
- some metals
- some gems

What Are Minerals Like?

- Some make marks.
- All break.
- Some are hard.
- Some are soft.
- Some are shiny.
- Some are dull.
- Some are colorful.
- Some are crystals.

Where Do People Find Minerals?

- in food
- in the sea
- in the ground
- in mines

Glossary

crystals the regular shapes of minerals

*Some minerals are **crystals**.*

gems beautiful, rare minerals

*Some minerals are **gems**.*

metals minerals that conduct energy

*Some minerals are **metals**.*

minerals solid natural materials of many colors and types

***Minerals** are old.*

rocks solid parts of Earth's crust
*Minerals are in **rocks**.*

solids matter that has shape
*Minerals are **solids**.*

Index

crystals, 13
dull, 11
food, 14
gems, 7
ground, 6, 16
hard, 10
metals, 7
minerals, 2, 4–18
mines, 17
old, 4
rocks, 5
sea, 15
shiny, 11
soft, 10
solids, 4